famous spies

Union spy Lafayette Baker crosses Bull Run under Confederate fire.

A Pull Ahead Book

famous spies

Frank Surge

Lerner Publications Company • Minneapolis, Minnesota

ACKNOWLEDGMENTS: The illustrations are reproduced through the courtesy of: pp. 2, 6, 11, 19, 20, 21, 28, 30, 35, 36, 37, 49, 51, Independent Picture Service; pp. 5, 26, 27, 29, 34, 44, 46, Chicago Historical Society; p. 9, Crown Publishers; p. 10, Louvre, Paris, Photograph Giraudon; p. 13, Metropolitan Museum of Art; p. 15, Culver Pictures, Inc.; pp. 16, 40, Library of Congress; p. 22, Bettmann Archive; p. 31, *Dictionary of American Portraits,* Dover Publications, Inc.; pp. 32, 39, 54, National Archives; p. 38, Ishbel Ross; p. 42, New York Public Library, Manuscripts Division; p. 43, Valentine Museum; p. 45, Museum of Fine Arts, Boston; p. 50, Radio Times Hulton Picture Library; p. 52, A. A. Hoehling.

Second Printing 1970

Standard Book Number: 8225-0454-5
Library of Congress Catalog Number: 68-30569

contents

Belle Boyd
(Courtesy Chicago Historical Society)

Samson and Delilah

Delilah

The history of espionage contains many stories of glamorous women spies. One of the first of these, Delilah, was hired by the Philistines to spy on her lover, Samson, the ruler and strong man of Israel. Her job: to find out what made Samson strong.

"Use all your arts to find out his secret," they said, "and we will each give you eleven hundred pieces of silver."

That night Delilah went to Samson and used her arts. Then she asked him, "Samson, what makes you so strong? What could a man tie you with if he wanted you at his mercy?"

"Seven strands of gut, still fresh and undried," said Samson.

So the Philistines brought Delilah some fresh wet gut, and she tied Samson with it when he was sleeping. Then she yelled, "Samson, the Philistines!" And Samson broke his bonds.

"This time tell me the truth," said Delilah. "What bonds can hold you?"

"New ropes that have never been used," said Samson.

So again Delilah bound him, and again she yelled, "Samson, the Philistines!" And again he broke loose.

"Another lie!" exclaimed Delilah. "This time tell me what the right bonds are."

"Weave seven of the hairs on my head into your web and tie them to the peg of the loom and make it fast in the ground," said Samson.

Again Delilah did as he said, and again she yelled, "Samson, the Philistines!" And Samson got up with the whole loom hanging from his head.

"I hate deceitful people," said Delilah. And she nagged Samson so much that he finally gave in and told her.

"My strength is in my hair, which has never been cut. If my hair were cut, my strength would be gone."

So Delilah had her servant bring in a razor, and she cut Samson's hair while he slept. His strength left him. She tied him, and then yelled, as before, "Samson, the Philistines!" This time he couldn't get away. They blinded him and put him to work as a prisoner. But they forgot that hair grows again after it's been cut.

Samson leans on the pillars.

After a while, the Philistine leaders met to praise their god and have a feast. They brought in Samson and had him stand where they could point and laugh at him. He asked his guide to lead him to the two pillars that supported the building, so that he could lean against them and rest. He put one hand on each pillar and shook them with such force that the whole building collapsed, crushing Samson and the whole crowd of Philistines. Perhaps Delilah was also in the building.

Mithridates VI of Pontus.
From a coin in the Louvre, Paris.

Mithridates VI

At the age of 11, in about 120 B.C., Mithridates VI became the king of Pontus, an area in Asia Minor which is now part of modern Turkey. After his mother tried to murder him several times, the boy king, feeling unwanted and insecure, fled into exile in the mountains. During the next few years he became a hunter and a spy. He traveled around Asia Minor disguised as a caravan boy. On his travels he mastered 22 languages and dialects and learned the customs and military strength of the different tribes. He returned to his homeland, defeated his mother and two brothers, and took over the throne. He had enjoyed his travels so much that he decided to revisit all the places he had seen. This time he took an army with him and conquered as he went along.

A Roman general addresses his troops before battle. Mithridates fought three major wars with the Roman republic between 83 B.C. and 63 B.C.

He murdered his mother, his sons, and his sister, who was also his wife. He murdered his harem to prevent his enemies from enjoying it. He was always suspicious, always afraid that someone would try to take the throne from him. Most of all, he feared the Romans, who were trying to gain territory in the East. He massacred 100,000 Roman subjects who lived in Asia Minor, and fought against the famous Roman generals, Lucullus and Pompey. He continued to plot against the Romans until the end of his life. The end came while he was forming a league of tribes in a plan to invade Italy. He was poisoned by a son he had forgotten to murder.

Dominique Cartouche

Dominique Cartouche was a French outlaw leader who organized an underworld army of spies. This spy network enabled him to commit large-scale robbery and avoid the police.

In October 1693 Francois Louis Cartouche, a Paris saddle-maker, registered the birth of a son, Louis Dominique. Years later, after the son's death, he revealed that Dominique was really the son of a nobleman who had paid Cartouche to raise the boy as his own. At the age of 14, Dominique was sent to a Jesuit school, where he was snubbed by the other boys. He ran away and joined a troupe of strolling acrobats. And from there he moved into an underworld career.

He was a good actor. He could change his appearance and identity. He could pass himself off as a soldier, a noble, a gambler, or whatever else he chose to be. He recruited bank clerks, merchants, and police to serve as his agents

Costume Studies by Claude Gillot (1673-1722). Cartouche's career began among strolling players like those in Gillot's drawing. *(Metropolitan Museum of Art, Rogers Fund, 1909)*

and informers. He had as many as 2,000 spies working for him in Paris. He bribed prison guards, court officials, and even doctors, whom he hired to treat his wounded men. When the police declared that there was no such person as Cartouche, he began to make public appearances and mock the police. He had 20 of his men disguised as himself, and told them to appear in different parts of Paris at the same time. He stole plate, jewels, and silver candlesticks from the palace. With the police unable to catch him, the military was called in, but he continued to rob and get away with it. Finally one of his men gave in to bribery, and he was captured.

Dominique was convinced that he would escape. He had spies and agents in every prison. He resisted every torture that was used in attempts to make him confess. But it gradually became clear to him that his followers had deserted him. About to be executed, he avenged himself by telling everything about his spy system and naming all his accomplices. They included half the tradesmen of Paris and all the tavern-keepers. Four hundred men were arrested and executed.

In prison, Dominique Cartouche (left) names his accomplices.

Nathan Hale

Nathan Hale

Nathan Hale is remembered because, when the British hanged him as a spy, he met his death proudly and bravely. If he had been a better spy, he might not have been hanged.

He was born in 1755 and died by hanging in September 1776 at the age of 21. He was born in Coventry, Connecticut, one of 12 children. As a boy he was intelligent, athletic, handsome, and cool-natured. He entered Yale in 1769 and graduated in 1773. He taught school for a year in Connecticut. Then, when the Revolution broke out, he became a part of it. In July 1775 he received a lieutenant's commission and fought in the siege of Boston. After that he was transfered to New York and made a captain.

He became a member of a small group called the Rangers, who were respected for their fighting qualities and daring leadership on dangerous missions. General George Washington asked the Ranger commander to choose a man to pass through British lines to get information about the British positions. When the commander asked for a volunteer, he got Nathan Hale.

Nathan was doomed to fail. He was inexperienced and untrained in spying. He could be easily spotted and remembered, because his face had been scarred by exploding powder. His mission was poorly planned. There was no planned cover, no arrangement for contact with American civilians behind British lines. Apparently he was not given money. No line of communication was set up. He would have to write out his information and carry it with him. The plans were not kept secret. Every officer in the Rangers knew that he was going out to spy. He talked over his plans with a friend. When he left, there was no explanation of his disappearance. He just went.

A sloop dropped him off on Long Island. Still in uniform, he changed to a brown suit. He was to pretend to be a Dutch schoolmaster. He got the information General Washington wanted, but on the night of September 21, 1776, he was arrested. When he was questioned, he lost his cool. He became so flustered that he was easily trapped. The British commander, General Howe, ordered him to be hanged the next morning without a trial. When he asked for a minister and a Bible, the jailer refused his request.

In the morning a noose was thrown over the limb of a tree. Nathan Hale, with his arms bound, stumbled up a ladder. The noose was put around his neck. The ladder was pulled out from under him. His body was left hanging there as a warning to others.

The execution of Nathan Hale. New York City, September 1776.

His last words were a quotation from a popular play about a Roman statesman, *Cato,* by Joseph Addison: "I only regret that I have but one life to lose for my country."

Karl Schulmeister

Karl Schulmeister

Karl Schulmeister was Napoleon's favorite spy. He was one of the most effective and daring of all spies. He was clever, bold, physically strong, and energetic. He was a good actor.

Karl was born on August 5, 1770, in Alsace, a province in eastern France near the German border. His father was a Lutheran clergyman. By the time he was 17 Karl was a successful, wealthy smuggler. By 1804 he was a secret agent. After the French Revolution a law had been passed stating that any nobles who left the country would be executed if they returned. Karl received $30,000 for luring a Bourbon prince back into France, where he was arrested and executed.

In 1805 Karl became a full-scale spy for Napoleon. At that time Napoleon was at war with Austria. Karl was sent

Napoleon Bonaparte, emperor of France. Schulmeister's information helped Napoleon defeat Austrian and Russian forces at the battle of Austerlitz, December 1805.

to Vienna to spy on an Austrian officer, Marshal Mack. He pretended to be a Hungarian noble who had been kicked out of France because he was suspected of spying for Austria. Mack befriended him and took him around into the exclusive army clubs of Vienna. He made Karl a part of his personal staff. Soon he was serving as Mack's chief spy. He managed to inform Napoleon of every enemy move.

Vienna in the 1790's. Capital of the Austrian empire, the city was occupied by Napoleon in 1805 and again in 1809.

Karl spoke French, German, and Hungarian. He had a pleasant personality and was easily able to pass for an officer and a gentleman in Austrian society. Everyone liked him.

He bribed two Austrian officers so that, when he gave Mack false information, they backed him up. He convinced Mack that France was falling apart and wouldn't be able to fight a war. Napoleon had a newspaper especially printed with false news about France, and Karl showed this newspaper to Mack. Mack believed that the French army was withdrawing to put down rebellion in France. He went out to pursue the retreating French army and found his own army surrounded. He surrendered.

Karl remained in Vienna and continued to mislead the Austrians and Russians. Finally he was exposed and arrested. He was rescued when the French occupied Vienna. All this time he had been receiving pay from both France and Austria. Under the French occupation of Vienna, he was appointed censor of plays, publishing houses, and religious establishments. By 1807 he was a very rich man.

He continued to serve Napoleon until 1810, when Napoleon married the Austrian Archduchess Marie Louise. She brought Austrian influence to Paris, and Karl had to retire. After Napoleon's defeat the Austrian artillery destroyed Karl's home in Alsace. When Napoleon escaped from Elba, Karl joined him again. When Napoleon was finally defeated at Waterloo, Karl was one of the first to be arrested. He saved himself by paying a huge ransom. He tried to regain his wealth by speculating in business ventures, but he lost everything. He was still popular in Alsace, and managed to make his living running a tobacco shop granted to him by the government. He died in 1853, poor but happy.

Lafayette C. Baker

Lafayette Baker was one of the first professional spies in the United States. He is one of the few spies in earlier American history who is studied and respected by people who study and respect professional spies.

In April 1861 he reported to General Winfield Scott in Washington and volunteered to penetrate Confederate lines to discover military secrets of the Southern army. Scott gave him ten 20-dollar gold pieces and set him on his way. The appointment was not official. Baker went uncommissioned and unarmed.

He carried a camera and pretended to be a traveling photographer. In those days a man with a camera did not arouse suspicions, as he would today. The camera was a new fad, a novelty not really thought of as a tool for spying. A traveling photographer was looked upon more as a minstrel or a strolling actor. No one bothered to check his camera. If they did, they would have found out that it didn't even work.

On July 11, 1861, Baker started for Richmond. He didn't get very far. He was captured trying to get through the Federal lines, by Federal soldiers who had no idea who he was or what he was doing. They sent him back to General Scott, who said: "Leave him to me. I'll deal with him." Scott dealt with him by sending him off toward Richmond again. This time he was caught trying to sneak through with a regiment of Federal soldiers and was again sent back to General Scott.

Confederate general
Pierre Beauregard
(Courtesy Chicago Historical Society)

On the third try he made it within Confederate lines. Two Confederate soldiers caught him and arrested him as a spy. They were friendly Confederate soldiers; they asked him to have a beer with them. Several beers later the two soldiers fell asleep, and Baker continued on his way to Richmond. Then four cavalrymen captured him and sent him to General Bonham, who sent him to General Beauregard, who put him in the care of a guard, who gave him a tour of the area. Now he had important information for General Scott but no way to send it.

Then General Beauregard sent him to Jefferson Davis in Richmond. Baker had been claiming to be Sam Munson from Knoxville, Tennessee. Now a man from Knoxville was

Union general
Winfield Scott
(Courtesy Chicago Historical Society)

brought in to identify him. Baker heard the man referred to as Mr. Brock. When Brock entered the room, Baker greeted him and, knowing a little about Knoxville, bluffed Brock into thinking he should know him. The bluff worked. Baker was placed under parole and allowed to wander about Richmond. He got information about military plans and troop movements. Then, after managing to get a pass from a provost marshal, he left Richmond. Soon Confederate soldiers were after him. He slept under some hay in a barn. When the soldiers searched the barn they missed him. He made it to the Potomac, stole a rowboat, and rowed across while Confederate soldiers shot at him from behind. On the other side of the Potomac he fell exhausted

Lafayette Baker (right) meets Jefferson Davis, President of the Confederacy. Richmond, 1861.

and lay there until a farmer picked him up. The next morning he arrived in Washington and pushed his way into General Scott's office. First he was fed, and then he made his report.

Baker later had charge of his own corps of espionage and counter-espionage agents. He then became an agent in the secret service of the war department. As a secret service agent his most important job was to protect the life of President Lincoln. He failed.

Belle Boyd *(Courtesy Chicago Historical Society)*

Belle Boyd

Many people believe that Belle Boyd was the most glamorous and remarkable of the Civil War spies. The first person to believe this was Belle Boyd. She believed it so strongly that after the war she traveled the country giving lectures about her experiences. People paid to listen to her.

Lafayette Baker and Belle Boyd. Miss Boyd is peddling religious tracts among Union prisoners at a rebel stockade.

She started her career as a Confederate agent in July 1861 in Martinsburg, Virginia, now West Virginia. A Union soldier tried to raise a flag over the Boyd house. When Mrs. Boyd tried to slam the door in his face, he pushed it open again. Belle, who was 17 at the time, drew out a pistol and killed him. Such an accomplishment made her big-headed, and she decided to become a spy.

Confederate general
Stonewall Jackson.

Belle seemed to be able to get much information with little effort. She listened to the gossip of Federal officers. She became expert in using secret codes and supplying Southern armies with information about Northern troop movements. In May 1862, wearing a dark blue dress, a white sunbonnet, and a small frilled apron, she set out with information for Stonewall Jackson. She ran through crowds of Union infantry and through the lines under heavy fire. Jackson won the battle.

She was captured when she gave a message for Jackson to a man in Confederate gray who turned out to be a Union spy. A secret service detective named Cridge was sent to escort her to Washington. He resisted her romantic charms,

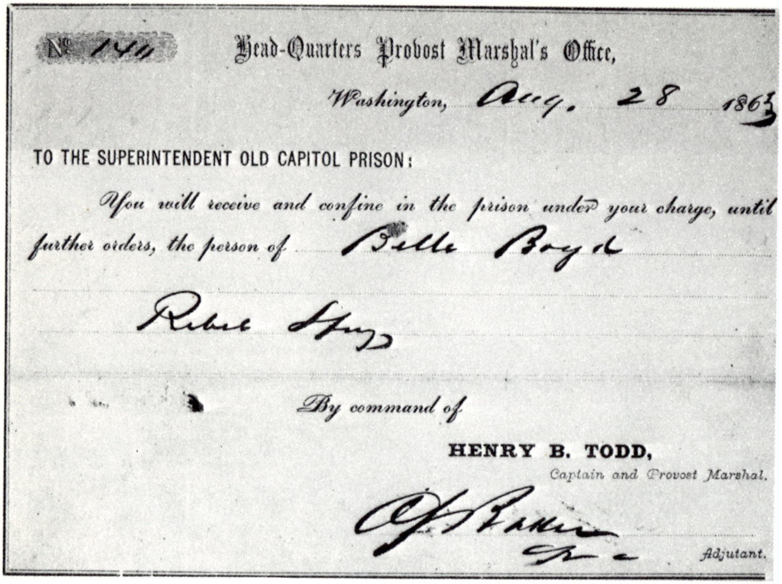
№ 141 Head-Quarters Provost Marshal's Office,

Washington, Aug. 28 1863

TO THE SUPERINTENDENT OLD CAPITOL PRISON:

You will receive and confine in the prison under your charge, until further orders, the person of Belle Boyd

Rebel Spy

By command of

HENRY B. TODD,
Captain and Provost Marshal.

[illegible]
Adjutant.

Belle Boyd was captured by a Union spy and sent to prison in Washington, D.C. Above, her identification papers.

and she became a prisoner in Washington. Eventually she was released in a prisoner exchange and escorted to Richmond, where she was serenaded by a city band.

Later, at sea, Belle met Sam Wylde Hardinge, a Federal naval officer. They fell in love, and he resigned his commission to marry her. They lived in England until Hardinge's early death. In England Belle wrote her autobiography, *Belle Boyd in Camp and Prison,* in which she exaggerated herself and her accomplishments. After the war she became an actress and returned to the United State to give dramatic lectures about her experiences. She married twice more.

Emma Edmonds

Emma Edmonds was a Canadian-born nurse whose family had moved to the United States. On April 12, 1861, the day of the firing on Fort Sumter, she was in New York. She immediately volunteered as a nurse for the Union army. She was stationed with General McClellan's forces near Yorktown when McClellan received word that a Federal spy was to be shot in Richmond. Emma was suggested to replace him as a spy. A phrenologist studied the shape of her head and declared that she would make a good spy.

She dressed herself as a Negro field hand. The company barber shaved her head, and she put on a curly wig. She darkened her skin. To test her disguise she went to the company doctor with whom she had worked and asked for a job as a handyman. She was not recognized. After sneaking through the enemy lines, she was immediately picked up and put to work doing hard physical labor with pick, shovel, and wheelbarrow. She made sketches and wrote descriptions of what she saw. On the second day a fellow worker commented that she seemed to be getting lighter. Her answer was that she had always expected to turn white some day, since her mother was a white woman. The next night she returned to the Federal lines and made her report. Then she bleached her skin and returned to nursing.

A group of contraband slaves rest on a farm in Cumberland, Maryland, 1862. Contrabands were Southern slaves who escaped to or beyond Union lines during the Civil War. *(Courtesy Chicago Historical Society)*

Emma Edmonds disguised as a contraband.

For her next expedition she disguised herself as an Irish peddler-woman, selling pastries and knick-knacks. She crossed the Chickahominy River on horseback and sent her horse back across the river. She had to spend the night in the swamp. She, her food, and her hospital quilt were soaked. She came down with chills and fever and couldn't move for three days. She finally got through the swamp and came to a deserted house. Entering the house, she found a rebel soldier lying on a straw tick, sick with typhoid and half-starved. She cared for him. He told her that his name was Allan Hall and asked her to deliver his gold watch to Major McKee. Then he died.

Emma prepares tea and hoe-cake for a sick rebel.

In the house Emma found mustard, pepper, an old pair of green spectacles, and a bottle of red ink. She decided to improve her disguise. She made a mustard plaster the size of a silver dollar and tied it on one side of her face. When it blistered she cut off the blister and put on a large patch of black courtplaster. With the ink she painted red lines around her eyes. She darkened her complexion with ochre. She rubbed the black pepper in her eyes to make them red and watery. She put on the green glasses and her Irish hood and left for the rebel lines. She went to Major McKee's headquarters, but the Major was out on a scouting expedition. While awaiting his return, she spent her time peddling

Another perilous escape, this time on a stolen colt.

and spying. When she saw Major McKee she told him about "her dearest friend," Captain Hall. She offered to take him to the body in exchange for a horse. When she got the horse she rode away to the Federal lines.

Emma Edmonds made nine other spy trips, using different disguises. When the Union forces occupied Louisville, she was promoted from spy to detective. She served in Louisville as a counterspy, discovering and revealing Confederate spies. At Vicksburg she fell ill with a fever and lost her strength. She was given a certificate of disability and commended for her heroic services.

She recorded her experiences in a book, *Nurse and Spy*.

The Wild Rose, in her thirties.

Rose O'Neale Greenhow

Rose O'Neale, born in Maryland in 1817, grew up to be the belle of Washington. She was a tall, dark, beautiful woman and a cultured person. Attractive to men, she was nicknamed The Wild Rose. She married Dr. Robert Greenhow and became an influential woman in Washington. In

1857, while the Greenhow family was traveling in California, Dr. Greenhow fell down a grating and died. Later a daughter, Gertrude, also died. Back in Washington, Rose was visited often by President James Buchanan.

After Lincoln became President in 1861, Thomas Jordan, a lieutenant from Virginia, resigned from the army to join the Confederacy. Jordan suggested that Rose become a spy for the South, and she followed his suggestion. The information that she sent to General Beauregard played a part in the Southern victory at Bull Run. She sent detailed information about Washington's defenses to Southern leaders in Richmond.

It wasn't long before she was suspected of being a spy, but proof was needed. Allan Pinkerton, head of the secret service, was brought in to trail her. Pinkerton spied on her by taking off his shoes and standing on the shoulders of one of his men, so that he could look through her window.

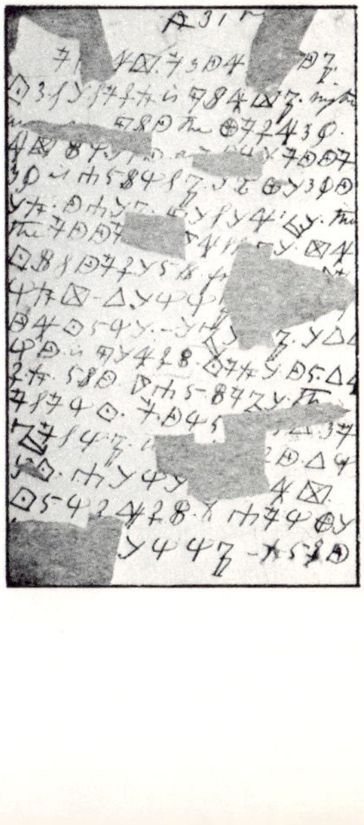

A letter in code from Rose Greenhow to Thomas Jordan.

He got his proof, and on August 23, 1861, she was arrested. He tried to use her house as a trap for other rebel spies, but with no success. While he and his men were waiting in the house, Rose's eight-year-old daughter was sitting in a tree near the house singing a little song. The words to the song were: "Mother has been arrested, Mother has been arrested." Rose was deported to the South. President Lincoln considered this adequate punishment.

Mrs. Greenhow and her daughter Rose in Old Capitol Prison, Washington, D.C., 1862. They were released after six months' imprisonment.

Elizabeth Van Lew

Elizabeth Van Lew—"Crazy Bet"—was the Union's most valuable spy against the South during the Civil War. She lived in Richmond, Virginia, but she hated slavery. She favored the Union and her neighbors knew it. She helped runaway slaves and she hid escaped Yankee prisoners. Her neighbors suspected these things, but they did not suspect that she was also a Yankee spy.

Elizabeth was born in Richmond in 1818. She was sent to school in Philadelphia, her mother's hometown. When she returned to Richmond she was an abolitionist. She freed nine of the family slaves. She tried to find and buy the husbands or wives of slaves her family owned, so that families would be together. She got away with this behavior in Richmond because her family was of high social standing.

She was in her early 40's when the Civil War broke out. At once she began sending letters to Washington reporting what was going on in Richmond. While other women knitted for Virginia's soldiers, Elizabeth worked on intelligence reports for the North. She went to Libby Prison and tended wounded Yankee prisoners there. The prisoners gave her information from the combat zone, hidden in food baskets, medicine bottles, or books she had lent them. No one was suspicious because she encouraged the idea that she was, indeed, "Crazy Bet," as the citizens of Richmond called her.

Elizabeth Van Lew (right) dines with her family in the garden.

By this time her father had died and her brother had married. She and her mother, also an abolitionist, lived alone with the servants. Confederate officers and government officials continued visiting the Van Lew mansion, and Elizabeth continued getting information from them. When her permit to visit the prisoners was revoked, she would go to an official and flatter him into giving her a new one.

One of her agents was Mary Elizabeth Bowser, a slave she had helped and educated. She got Mary Elizabeth a job as a waitress in the home of Confederate President Jefferson Davis, where the girl spied and reported information without ever being suspected.

Elizabeth
Van Lew

Libby Prison, Richmond, Virginia. The building had been a tobacco warehouse before the war. *(Courtesy Chicago Historical Society)*

Elizabeth made up a private code for her messages. When she sent servants out with baskets of eggs, every basket contained one hollow shell with a message in it. The Van Lew seamstress always had messages hidden among her goods. Sometimes Elizabeth sent flowers to General Grant with messages in them. And still she wasn't caught. Her brother John knew what she was doing, but he kept his mouth shut. When he was drafted into the Confederate army, he deserted and was hidden by Union sympathizers.

During the war a total of 109 men escaped by tunnel from Libby Prison. When a prisoner escaped he went immediately to the Van Lews' home, where he was hidden in a secret guest room. The room was so secret it is not even mentioned in Elizabeth's diary. Her niece told about this room years later. One night she saw "Aunt Betty" going somewhere with a big platter of food. She followed. Elizabeth stood before a black hole in the wall. A shaggy, bearded man in a worn blue uniform was reaching out for the food. The girl didn't tell what she saw. Later she went up by herself, found the secret panel, and talked to the soldier.

Thousands of captured Union officers died in Libby Prison. *(Painting by David G. Blythe (1815-1865). Courtesy, Museum of Fine Arts, Boston)*

Jefferson Davis, President of the Confederacy. *(Courtesy Chicago Historical Society)*

A few days before the fall of Richmond, Elizabeth smuggled a large American flag into the house. When the Federal troops appeared, she raised the first Union flag that announced the surrender of Richmond.

When Grant became President, he made Elizabeth postmistress of Richmond, but she was shut out socially. She never received any pay for her services or for any of the money she spent on her spying. After Grant left office, she was dismissed. She spent her last years in poverty, living on a pension from northern friends and attended by her loyal Negro servants.

Wilhelm Stiebur

Wilhelm Stiebur of Prussia was called "the spymaster" and "the king of sleuth-hounds." He had no conscience or sense of shame. Therefore he was able to serve his country well.

He was born on May 3, 1818, in Prussian Saxony. His family moved to Berlin, where he began to study for the Lutheran ministry. But before long he changed his plans and became a lawyer. In 1845 he was already a spy and stool pigeon. He turned in a labor agitator named Schloeffel, who was his wife's uncle. He posed as a friend of the workingman, so that he could spy on liberals and radicals. Between 1845 and 1850 he built up a successful law practice. He concentrated on criminal cases. He was admired for the brilliance with which he defended his clients, until it was learned that he was also editor of the police periodical. In this position he was able to know in advance what evidence would be produced against his clients in court. In spite of the scandal, King Frederick William remained loyal to him and appointed him commissioner of police.

In 1851 Stiebur went to England to spy on Karl Marx and other German radicals, but the British government wouldn't cooperate with him. He went to Paris and, by pretending to be a friend of Socialists and liberals, got a list of the names of radicals still in Germany. Then he went home and began arresting large numbers of people, causing many Germans to flee to America. When he intercepted and read the letters they sent back to Germany, he became furious at their praise of the freedom they found in America.

When William I became ruler of Prussia, Stiebur was dismissed. Now all his enemies turned on him and brought him to trial. He proved that all the rotten things he had done were done at the king's command. The court couldn't convict him without also condemning his employer, Frederick William, who was in a sanitarium. Between 1858 and 1863 Stiebur worked for the Tsar of Russia, helping to organize the Tsar's secret police service. He worked with the foreign branch of this service, tracing Russian criminals

Otto von Bismarck, chancellor of Prussia.

after they had left Russia. Even though he was no longer employed by Prussia, he continued spying for Prussia while he was working for Russia. In 1863 he met Bismarck, chancellor of Prussia, who was planning to conquer Austria. He went to Austria to spy for Bismarck. Pretending to be a peddler, he drove around Austria with a horse and wagon, selling religious statues and dirty pictures. Largely because of the information he collected, Prussia conquered Austria easily. Other Prussian officials hated Stiebur, but every time they showed their hatred Chancellor Bismarck rewarded him with a promotion. He handled several jobs: protecting the king and Bismarck, controlling military censorship, and turning out propaganda. He organized a Central Information Bureau and set up his own news bureau. The king now liked him, and gave him rewards and honors.

Next he spent 18 months spying in France, preparing for the Franco-Prussian War. He and his agents brought home three trunkloads of information, which they checked on the train like any other luggage. He claimed he had 40,000 spies in France. They spied not only on the military but also on civilians. During the Franco-Prussian War, he severely punished Frenchmen suspected of spying on the Prussian invaders. Peasants were strung up and tortured to death just for looking at an ammunition train. A young bridegroom was executed for keeping a diary.

The Prussian infantry launch an attack upon the French, 1870.

In January 1871, William I went to Versailles to proclaim Germany an empire, and himself emperor.

Stiebur showed no respect toward anyone except the king and Bismarck. He became more and more cruel and arrogant. He also continued to become more powerful. He set up networks of railroad spies and hotel spies, and tried to get into banking and international business. He bought newspapers in neighboring countries and published pro-German propaganda. As minister of police he continued protecting Bismarck and the king from would-be assassins. He opened an establishment in Berlin called The Green House, and then kept a blackmail file on the people who came there.

In 1882 he was stricken with arthritis and died. Many distinguished people attended his funeral.

Alice Dubois

Alice Dubois

In August 1914 many French refugees, fleeing ahead of the German invasion of their country, managed to cross the channel into England. One of these refugees was an attractive, intelligent woman named Louise de Bettignies. She spoke English, German, and Italian, as well as her native French. She brought to England messages containing military information that had been entrusted to her by French officials. She also had information taken from her own observations. She was invited to London and asked if she would like to go back to France and organize a system of espionage.

Disguised as a maker and seller of laces, and calling herself Alice Dubois, she returned to her home town of Lille, France, and began to organize. Among her agents were a chemist, who forged passports; a mapmaker, Paul Bernard, who at one time wrote in coded shorthand a 1,600-word spy report to fit beneath the stamp on a post card; and Marie-Leonie Vanhoutte, who, as Charlotte the cheese peddler, roamed with Alice the lace peddler to gather information. Eventually the group had 40 members. Alice crossed into Holland once a week with information the group collected.

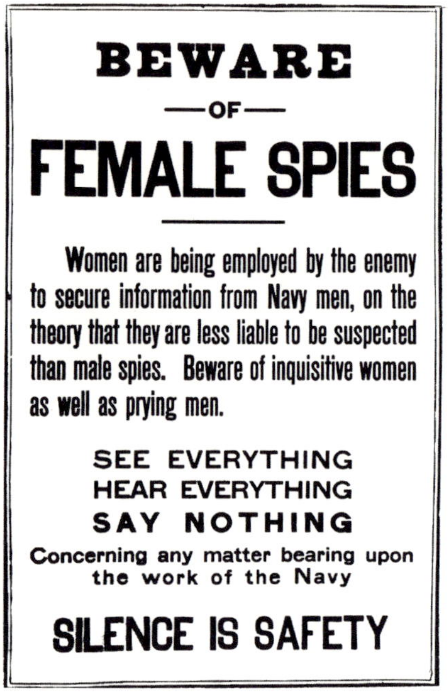

Spy fever hit America during World War I. This warning poster came from the Navy.

She worked out many methods of sending messages. She signaled with carillon bells. She hid messages in cakes of chocolate, toys, umbrellas, a lame man's wooden leg, and balls of yarn. Once she carried a message written in invisible ink on transparent paper placed beneath the glossy surface of a photograph. She hid a map in the rim of a pair of glasses.

During one of Alice's trips into Holland, Charlotte received a message telling her to hurry to a certain inn "on account of Alice." She knew that it might be a trap, but not wanting to show that she had anything to hide, she went to the inn. There she was questioned by an informer. She pretended not to know anyone named Alice, and informed the informer that he had the wrong person. The next day Charlotte was arrested by German secret agents. When Alice returned she was trailed for a few days and finally arrested. Both women were convicted and sentenced to death, but at the last minute the death sentences were changed to 27 years' imprisonment for Alice and 15 years for Charlotte. Alice died in prison on September 27, 1918, a few weeks before the war ended. Charlotte survived the war.

Mata Hari

Marguerite Gertrud Zelle was born in Leeuwarden, Holland, on August 7, 1876. When she was 18, she married Captain MacLeod, a 50-year-old Dutch officer of Scottish descent. She went to live with him in Java, a Dutch colony in the South Pacific, where he was stationed. MacLeod was a heavy drinker. He beat her, threatened her with a gun, and often chased around with other women. After six years she left him and went back to Holland. She left her daughter, Marie Louise, with relatives there and went to Paris. In Paris she began a new life as a different person. To entertain herself in Java she had studied and learned native dances. Now that she had to earn her own living, she made use of this learning. Calling herself Mata Hari (the eye of morning) and claiming to be from southern India, she worked up an act based on the Javanese dances. She earned her living by touring the European cities doing this act. She was a hit. Men pursued her. She became wealthy and was able to buy jewels and fine clothes, things she had never had before.

Mata Hari

Some of her men friends were important German officers. They would spend money on her and charge it to the German secret service. That is how her name appeared on lists as a German agent. She was not a trained spy, and any information she might have given these men was probably harmless. In France, when the French suspected her, she offered to spy for them against the Germans. In England, when the English suspected her, she claimed to be a French spy sent to spy on England. In Spain she spent more time with German officers. Back in France she was arrested and brought to trial. She claimed that the money she had received was not for spying. Many people believed her. They believed that she was only a foolish woman rather than a dangerous spy. But she was sentenced to be shot.

On October 15, 1917, Mata Hari faced the firing squad. Refusing the blindfold, she met her death bravely and calmly.

Banda

After her death Mata Hari became a legend that has remained alive through the years. Recently the legend has been given a new twist in the story of a woman who is said to have been the daughter of Mata Hari. This is the story that is told:

In October 1917, a 17-year-old girl in Java received a farewell letter from her mother. The girl's name was Banda. Her mother was Marguerite Gertrud Zelle MacLeod, Mata Hari. Her father was an Indonesian whom she never knew. She never discussed this letter with anyone except her foster-parents. She did not want people to know that she was the daughter of Mata Hari.

Banda wanted to be a teacher. She was able to fulfill this ambition when a friend in the government gave her the money for a college education. She opened one-room schoolhouses throughout the Dutch East Indies. She enjoyed working with children. She was a charming, beautiful

Eurasian woman, accepted and liked by people of all nationalities. She was also rich. Her government friend had died and left her a fortune.

In 1939, the early days of World War II, her parties became gathering places for diplomats, spies, and journalists. Then came the bombing of Pearl Harbor, and soon the Japanese landed in Indonesia. Banda tried to continue teaching. She told her children that tyrants come and go but the world goes on. The Japanese did not like this teaching, and she was forced to stop. Then an uncle who worked for the Japanese paid her a call. He blackmailed her. He told her that if she didn't work for the Japanese he would expose her as the daughter of Mata Hari. She had to start giving her parties again and invite people she knew and people chosen by the Japanese. During this time she met and fell in love with a man who seemed to be working with the Japanese. When she learned that he was really a leader in the Indonesian underground, she, too, joined the underground movement. She became a much better spy than her mother had been. She helped the allies by getting valuable information about Japanese battle plans, troop concentrations, and ship movements.

In 1945 the Japanese left Indonesia and the British and Dutch came in. Banda and her friend favored Indonesian independence. The Dutch opposed it. In 1948 war broke between the Dutch and the Indonesians. Banda spied on the Dutch and worked for freedom for Indonesia. After her friend married another woman, she dedicated herself to promoting the Indonesian cause. She went to the United States and gave lectures and interviews. Then she returned to Indonesia and, with the help of wealthy American friends, continued to work for independence. Soon Indonesia was free.

By this time Banda was known and respected by American intelligence. American officials contacted her and persuaded her to accept a mission to spy on Communist China. She obtained much valuable information, including the fact that Chiang-Kai-Shek's cause was hopeless. In March 1950 she reported that the North Koreans were going to attack South Korea, but her warnings were ignored, and a few months later there was war in Korea. Then she was discovered. She was recognized by a former friend in the Indonesian underground who was now a Communist leader in North Korea.

Mata Hari's daughter was arrested and shot without a trial. Perhaps before she died she remembered the words from her mother's letter: "War has its own brutal laws."

the author

Frank Surge is a native of Buhl, Minnesota. He attended the University of Minnesota, where he received a B.S. in English and an M.A. in Education. He has taught high school English for several years in Minnesota and Illinois, and now works in the Publications Division of the Minnesota Department of Education. He lives in St. Paul.

The Pull Ahead Books

AMERICA'S FIRST LADIES
1789 to 1865

AMERICA'S FIRST LADIES
1865 to Present Day

FAMOUS SPIES

SINGERS OF THE BLUES

WESTERN LAWMEN

WESTERN OUTLAWS

PRESIDENTIAL LOSERS

PIRATES AND BUCCANEERS

FAMOUS CRIMEFIGHTERS